Brews & Bites: A Beer Cheese Revolution

S.R. Moore

Published by S.R. Moore, 2023.

BREWS & BITES: A BEER CHEESE REVOLUTION

First edition. October 31, 2023.

ISBN: 979-8215890462

Written by S.R. Moore.

Also by S.R. Moore

Mysteries of Lavender Lane
The Secret of Lavender Lane
The Book Club Conspiracy
The Mosaic Murders

Standalone
Pizza Artistry: The Canvas of Flavor
Brews & Bites: A Beer Cheese Revolution
Souper Fusion: A Globetrotter's Culinary Journey in a Bowl
Slices of Heaven: Sandwiches Redefined for the Modern Foodie
Advent Cookies Around the World: A Global Gastronomic Journey
Pasta for the Senses
Shamrock & Spoon: Modern Irish Cooking for Every Occasion

Table of Contents

Introduction

Welcome to "Brews & Bites: A Beer Cheese Revolution" – a cookbook designed to elevate your home entertaining game and unlock the secrets of creating irresistible beer cheese dishes. This cookbook is a celebration of the harmonious marriage between beer, cheese, and the delightful world of culinary exploration. We invite you to embark on a gastronomic journey where bold flavors, creativity, and an undeniable passion for good food collide.

The purpose of this cookbook is to guide you through the art of crafting dishes that incorporate the rich and savory allure of beer cheese. Whether you're hosting a casual get-together with friends, a cozy family dinner, or just indulging your own taste buds, "Brews & Bites" offers a collection of recipes that will leave your guests craving more. It's a testament to the idea that great food can be both comforting and exciting, familiar yet unexpected.

Within these pages, you'll find recipes that span the culinary spectrum, from creamy beer cheese soups that warm the soul to indulgent beer cheese desserts that conclude your meal with a sweet, savory twist. Our cookbook also features beer cheese dips, sliders, and a variety of main dishes that will showcase the versatility of this delectable condiment. Each recipe is meticulously crafted, ensuring your success in the kitchen, whether you're a seasoned chef or a novice cook.

As you explore "Brews & Bites," you'll find that we've taken care to provide optional variations and substitutions for many of the recipes, allowing you to tailor each dish to your personal preferences. We've also included helpful tips and notes for success, ensuring that you achieve the perfect balance of flavors, textures, and presentation.

So, whether you're a beer enthusiast, a cheese aficionado, or simply someone who appreciates the joy of sharing delicious food with loved ones, "Brews & Bites: A Beer Cheese Revolution" is here to inspire your culinary adventures and redefine the way you experience the irresistible charm of beer cheese-infused cuisine. It's time to don your apron, raise your glass, and embark on a flavorful journey that will leave your taste buds tingling and your guests eager for more. Cheers to the Beer Cheese Revolution!

Kitchen Essential

For Cooking the Recipes:

1. **Pots and Pans**: A variety of sizes, including saucepans, skillets, and a stockpot for soups and stews.

2. **Baking Sheets and Dishes**: For baking appetizers and desserts.

3. **Blender or Food Processor**: Essential for creating smooth beer cheese sauces and soups.

4. **Mixing Bowls**: Various sizes for mixing ingredients.

5. **Cutting Board and Knives**: To prepare and chop ingredients.

6. **Whisk**: For mixing and emulsifying sauces and dressings.

7. **Wooden Spatula and Tongs**: For stirring and flipping.

8. **Measuring Cups and Spoons**: To accurately measure ingredients.

9. **Immersion Blender**: Handy for blending soups directly in the pot.

10. **Grater**: For grating cheese or zest for desserts.

11. **Serving Platters and Dishes**: For a stylish presentation of your dishes.

For Tips on Stocking the Pantry:

1. **Beer Cheese Sauce**: The heart of the recipes. You can buy it pre-made or make your own with beer, cheese, and seasonings.

2. **Various Cheeses**: Stock up on a variety of cheeses, including sharp cheddar, Gouda, and cream cheese for different flavor profiles.

3. **Beer**: Have a selection of beer styles on hand to match your dishes. Stout, IPA, and lagers are good choices.

4. **Flour**: For thickening sauces and batters.

5. **Vegetables**: Keep onions, garlic, bell peppers, and other vegetables for adding flavor to your dishes.

6. **Spices and Herbs**: Essentials include paprika, cayenne, thyme, oregano, and fresh herbs for garnish.

7. **Broth**: Both chicken and vegetable broth are useful for soups and stews.

8. **Meat and Protein**: Stock your freezer with ground beef, chicken, or other proteins used in the main course recipes.

9. **Bread and Pasta**: For sliders and sandwiches, keep a variety of bread and pasta on hand.

10. **Pantry Staples**: Items like sugar, olive oil, vinegar, salt, and pepper are essential for most recipes.

11. **Fruits**: Keep fruits like apples, lemons, and berries for dessert recipes.

12. **Dairy**: Besides cheese, have milk, cream, and butter for creamier dishes.

13. **Nuts and Sweeteners**: Ingredients like nuts, honey, and chocolate are essential for dessert recipes.

14. **Dipping and Topping Ingredients**: Stock up on items like caramel, chocolate sauce, and whipped cream for dessert toppings.

15. **Non-Alcoholic Substitutes**: For beer, have non-alcoholic beer or stock your pantry with ingredients like chicken or vegetable broth for dishes where alcohol is used.

Having these tools, utensils, and ingredients in your kitchen will ensure you're well-prepared to create the delicious appetizers, main courses, sides, and desserts from "Brews & Bites: A Beer Cheese Revolution." Tailor your pantry to the specific recipes you plan to make, and you'll be ready to elevate your home entertaining game.

Cooking Tips and Techniques

Fundamental Cooking Techniques

1. Sautéing and Pan-Frying:

- Sautéing is cooking ingredients quickly in a small amount of oil over high heat, often used for onions, garlic, and veggies.

- Pan-frying involves cooking ingredients in a larger amount of oil, creating a crispy exterior, like when preparing sliders or crispy side dishes.

2. Boiling and Simmering:

- Boiling involves cooking ingredients in a large amount of water, like pasta.

- Simmering is cooking in liquid at a temperature just below boiling, ideal for soups and stews.

3. Baking and Roasting:

- Baking is cooking in a closed environment, often for desserts.

- Roasting involves cooking in an open environment, achieving a crispy exterior, ideal for meat and vegetables.

4. Grilling:

- Grilling imparts a smoky flavor to meat and vegetables and is perfect for sliders.

5. Mixing and Blending:

- Mixing involves combining ingredients, like batters for desserts.

- Blending is used to create smooth sauces, dips, and soups.

6. Frying:

- Frying is cooking ingredients submerged in hot oil, often used for appetizers like pretzel bites.

7. Baking and Broiling:

- Baking desserts like bread pudding.

- Broiling provides a high, direct heat source for browning and melting cheese.

Tips and Tricks for Success:

1. Read the Recipe:

- Start by reading the entire recipe before beginning to ensure you understand the steps and have all the ingredients and tools ready.

2. Mise en Place:

- Prepare and measure all ingredients (mise en place) before you start cooking. This will streamline the cooking process.

3. Temperature Control:

- Maintain the right cooking temperature. Use a thermometer for meats and ensure pans are preheated for sautéing and pan-frying.

4. Don't Crowd the Pan:

- When sautéing or pan-frying, avoid overcrowding the pan. Cook in batches if necessary to prevent steaming and achieve a crispy texture.

5. Season Properly:

- Season dishes throughout the cooking process. Taste and adjust as needed.

6. Deglaze:

- After sautéing, deglaze the pan with a liquid (e.g., wine or broth) to incorporate the flavorful bits stuck to the pan into your sauce.

7. Test for Doneness:

- Use a meat thermometer to check the internal temperature of proteins. Learn to recognize cues for doneness in vegetables and pasta.

8. Tasting as You Go:

- Taste your dishes throughout the cooking process to adjust seasonings and flavors.

9. Presentation:

- Presentation matters. Take the time to arrange and garnish your dishes for an appealing visual impact.

10. Experiment and Customize:

- Feel free to experiment with variations and substitutions based on your preferences or dietary needs.

11. Patience and Practice:

- Cooking is a skill that improves with practice. Don't be discouraged by mistakes, and have fun in the kitchen!

By mastering these fundamental cooking techniques and keeping these tips and tricks in mind, you'll be well on your way to creating delicious appetizers, main courses, sides, and desserts from "Brews & Bites: A Beer Cheese Revolution." Enjoy the process, and your culinary skills will continue to grow!

Beer Cheese Sauce

Ingredients:
- 2 tablespoons unsalted butter
- 2 tablespoons all-purpose flour
- 1 cup beer (choose a beer that complements your dish)
- 2 cups shredded sharp cheddar cheese
- 1/2 cup milk
- 1/4 teaspoon cayenne pepper (adjust to taste)
- Salt and black pepper to taste

Instructions:
1. In a saucepan, melt the butter over medium heat.
2. Add the all-purpose flour and whisk continuously to create a smooth roux. Cook for about 2-3 minutes until the roux is light golden in color.
3. Slowly pour in the beer while whisking vigorously to avoid lumps. Allow the mixture to simmer and thicken for about 2-3 minutes.
4. Reduce the heat to low and gradually add the shredded cheddar cheese while continuing to whisk. Make sure each addition of cheese is fully melted and incorporated before adding more.
5. Once the cheese is fully melted and the sauce is smooth, pour in the milk to achieve your desired consistency. You can adjust the amount of milk to make the sauce thicker or thinner.
6. Season the beer cheese sauce with cayenne pepper, salt, and black pepper. Adjust the seasonings to your taste preferences.
7. Simmer for a few more minutes, stirring occasionally, to ensure the sauce is well combined and heated through.

Appetizers

1. **Beer Cheese Stuffed Pretzel Bites**: Soft pretzel bites filled with a savory beer cheese filling, perfect for dipping.

2. **Beer Cheese Fondue**: A classic fondue made with a rich beer cheese blend, served with bread cubes, vegetables, and sausage for dipping.

3. **Beer Cheese Potato Skins**: Crispy potato skins loaded with a hearty beer cheese sauce, bacon, and green onions.

4. **Beer Cheese-Stuffed Mushrooms**: Larg=87exxxe mushroom caps filled with a creamy beer cheese mixture and baked until golden.

5. **Bavarian Beer Cheese Spread**: A flavorful spread made with cream cheese, beer, and a blend of spices, served with artisanal crackers.

6. **Beer Cheese-Stuffed Jalapeño Poppers**: Spicy jalapeño peppers filled with a zesty beer cheese filling, wrapped in bacon, and baked to perfection.

7. **Beer Cheese Bruschetta**: Slices of toasted baguette topped with a delightful beer cheese spread and fresh tomato salsa.

8. **Beer Cheese Fritters**: Bite-sized fritters made from a beer cheese batter, deep-fried to a golden crisp and served with a dipping sauce.

9. **Beer Cheese and Bacon Deviled Eggs**: Classic deviled eggs with a twist – a dollop of beer cheese and crumbled bacon on top.

10. **Beer Cheese and Sausage Stuffed Mini Peppers**: Mini sweet peppers stuffed with a mixture of beer cheese and crumbled sausage, then roasted until tender.

These appetizer recipes will add a delightful touch to your home entertaining and keep your guests coming back for more.

Beer Cheese Stuffed Pretzel Bites

Ingredients:
- 1 pound pizza dough
- 1 cup beer cheese sauce
- 1 egg (beaten, for egg wash)
- Coarse sea salt, for sprinkling

Instructions:
1. Preheat your oven to 375°F (190°C). Line a baking sheet with parchment paper.
2. Roll out the pizza dough into a rectangle, then cut it into bite-sized squares.
3. Place a small spoonful of beer cheese sauce in the center of each square, then fold the dough over to form a ball.
4. Brush the tops of the pretzel bites with beaten egg and sprinkle with sea salt.
5. Bake for 12-15 minutes or until they turn golden brown. Serve warm.

Preparation Time: 20 minutes
Cooking Time: 12-15 minutes
Yield: About 24 pretzel bites
Optional: Serve with additional beer cheese sauce for dipping.

Beer Cheese Fondue

Ingredients:
- 2 cups shredded cheddar cheese
- 1 cup shredded gruyere cheese
- 1 clove garlic, halved
- 1 cup beer (lager or ale)
- 1 tablespoon cornstarch
- 1 tablespoon lemon juice
- 1/2 teaspoon dry mustard
- 1 pinch nutmeg
- Cubed bread, steamed vegetables, and cooked sausage for dipping

Instructions:

1. In a bowl, toss the shredded cheese with cornstarch. Rub the inside of a fondue pot with the halved garlic.

2. Pour beer and lemon juice into the pot and heat over low-medium heat. Slowly add cheese, stirring constantly until it's melted and smooth.

3. Stir in dry mustard and a pinch of nutmeg.

4. Serve with cubed bread, steamed vegetables, and cooked sausage for dipping.

Preparation Time: 15 minutes

Cooking Time: 15 minutes

Yield: 4 servings

Optional: Use different types of bread or vegetables for dipping, and experiment with various beer styles for unique flavor profiles.

Beer Cheese Potato Skins

Ingredients:
- 4 large russet potatoes
- 1 cup beer cheese sauce
- 6 strips of bacon, cooked and crumbled
- 2 green onions, chopped
- Salt and pepper, to taste

Instructions:
1. Preheat your oven to 375°F (190°C).
2. Wash and scrub the potatoes. Bake them for 45-60 minutes until tender.
3. Cut the potatoes in half, scoop out the flesh, leaving about 1/4 inch of potato.
4. Brush the potato skins with oil, season with salt and pepper, and bake for another 10 minutes.
5. Fill each skin with beer cheese sauce, bacon, and green onions.
6. Bake for an additional 10 minutes or until the cheese is bubbly. Serve hot.

Preparation Time: 15 minutes
Cooking Time: 75-80 minutes (including potato baking time)
Yield: 8 potato skins

Beer Cheese-Stuffed Mushrooms

Ingredients:
- 24 large mushroom caps
- 1 cup beer cheese sauce
- 2 tablespoons breadcrumbs
- 2 tablespoons fresh parsley, chopped

Instructions:
1. Preheat your oven to 375°F (190°C). Remove the stems from the mushrooms.
2. Fill each mushroom cap with beer cheese sauce.
3. In a small bowl, combine breadcrumbs and chopped parsley.
4. Sprinkle the breadcrumb mixture on top of the cheese-filled mushrooms.
5. Place the mushrooms on a baking sheet and bake for 15-20 minutes until the mushrooms are tender and the topping is golden brown.

Preparation Time: 15 minutes
Cooking Time: 15-20 minutes
Yield: 24 stuffed mushrooms

Bavarian Beer Cheese Spread

Ingredients:
- 8 oz cream cheese, softened
- 1/2 cup beer cheese sauce
- 1/2 teaspoon garlic powder
- 1/2 teaspoon onion powder
- 1/4 teaspoon paprika
- 1/4 teaspoon cayenne pepper (adjust to taste)
- Assorted artisanal crackers

Instructions:
1. In a bowl, combine softened cream cheese and beer cheese sauce until well mixed.
2. Add garlic powder, onion powder, paprika, and cayenne pepper, and blend until smooth.
3. Serve the spread with a variety of artisanal crackers.

Preparation Time: 10 minutes

Yield: Approximately 1 1/2 cups of spread

Beer Cheese-Stuffed Jalapeño Poppers

Ingredients:
- 12 fresh jalapeño peppers
- 1 cup beer cheese sauce
- 12 slices of bacon

Instructions:
1. Preheat your oven to 375°F (190°C).
2. Cut the tops off the jalapeños and remove the seeds.
3. Fill each jalapeño with beer cheese sauce.
4. Wrap each stuffed jalapeño with a slice of bacon and secure with toothpicks.
5. Place on a baking sheet and bake for 20-25 minutes until the bacon is crispy and the peppers are tender.

Preparation Time: 20 minutes
Cooking Time: 20-25 minutes
Yield: 12 jalapeño poppers

Beer Cheese Bruschetta

Ingredients:
- Baguette, sliced into 1/2-inch thick rounds
- 1 cup beer cheese sauce
- 1 cup fresh tomato salsa
- Fresh basil leaves, for garnish

Instructions:
1. Preheat your oven to 375°F (190°C).
2. Toast the baguette slices in the oven until they are crisp and golden.
3. Spread beer cheese sauce on each toasted baguette round.
4. Top with fresh tomato salsa and garnish with fresh basil leaves.

Preparation Time: 15 minutes

Cooking Time: 5-10 minutes

Yield: Approximately 24 bruschettas

Beer Cheese Fritters

Ingredients:
- 1 cup all-purpose flour
- 1 teaspoon baking powder
- 1/2 teaspoon salt
- 1 cup beer cheese sauce
- 2 eggs
- Vegetable oil for frying

Instructions:

1. In a bowl, whisk together the flour, baking powder, and salt.

2. Add beer cheese sauce and eggs, and mix until smooth.

3. Heat vegetable oil in a deep pan or fryer to 350°F (175°C).

4. Drop spoonfuls of the batter into the hot oil and fry until they are golden brown and crispy.

5. Remove with a slotted spoon and drain on paper towels.

Preparation Time: 15 minutes

Cooking Time: 5-7 minutes (per batch)

Yield: Approximately 24 fritters

Beer Cheese and Bacon Deviled Eggs

Ingredients:
- 6 large eggs, hard-boiled and peeled
- 1/4 cup beer cheese sauce
- 2 slices of bacon, cooked and crumbled
- Paprika and chives for garnish

Instructions:
1. Cut the hard-boiled eggs in half and remove the yolks.
2. In a bowl, mash the egg yolks with beer cheese sauce until smooth.
3. Stir in half of the crumbled bacon.
4. Spoon or pipe the mixture back into the egg white halves.
5. Garnish with paprika, chives, and the remaining bacon.

Preparation Time: 20 minutes
Yield: 12 deviled egg halves

Beer Cheese and Sausage Stuffed Mini Peppers

Ingredients:
- 24 mini sweet peppers
- 1 cup beer cheese sauce
- 1/2 cup cooked and crumbled sausage

Instructions:
1. Preheat your oven to 375°F (190°C).
2. Cut the tops off the mini peppers and remove the seeds.
3. Fill each pepper with a mixture of beer cheese sauce and cooked sausage.
4. Place the stuffed peppers on a baking sheet and bake for 15-20 minutes until the peppers are tender and the filling is bubbly.

Preparation Time: 20 minutes
Cooking Time: 15-20 minutes
Yield: 24 stuffed mini peppers

Main Courses

1. **Beer Cheese-Stuffed Chicken Breasts**: Juicy chicken breasts stuffed with a flavorful beer cheese mixture, baked to perfection.

2. **Beer Cheese and Pretzel-Crusted Fish**: Crispy, beer cheese-coated fish fillets with a pretzel crust, served with a zesty dipping sauce.

3. **Beer Cheese Mac 'n' Cheese**: Creamy macaroni and cheese with a rich beer cheese sauce, baked until bubbly and golden.

4. **Beer Cheese Bratwurst Sandwiches**: Grilled bratwurst sausages served in a pretzel bun with beer cheese sauce, caramelized onions, and sauerkraut.

5. **Beer Cheese and Broccoli-Stuffed Potatoes**: Baked potatoes loaded with a cheesy beer cheese and broccoli mixture.

6. **Beer Cheese-Stuffed Burgers**: Juicy beef burgers filled with a gooey beer cheese center and served with your favorite toppings.

7. **Beer Cheese and Bacon-Wrapped Shrimp**: Succulent shrimp wrapped in bacon and brushed with a beer cheese glaze, then grilled to perfection.

8. **Beer Cheese and Bacon-Stuffed Mushrooms**: Large mushroom caps filled with a savory beer cheese and bacon mixture, roasted until golden.

9. **Beer Cheese Tacos**: Soft flour tortillas filled with beer cheese-coated grilled chicken or beef, topped with fresh salsa and avocado.

10. **Beer Cheese-Stuffed Meatloaf**: Classic meatloaf with a twist, stuffed with a hearty beer cheese filling and smothered in a beer cheese gravy.

These main dish recipes will elevate your home entertaining and delight your guests with the irresistible flavors of beer cheese.

Beer Cheese-Stuffed Chicken Breasts

Ingredients:

- 4 boneless, skinless chicken breasts
- 1 cup beer cheese sauce
- Salt and pepper, to taste
- Paprika, for garnish

Instructions:

1. Preheat your oven to 375°F (190°C).

2. Cut a pocket into each chicken breast and stuff with beer cheese sauce.

3. Season the chicken with salt and pepper and sprinkle paprika on top.

4. Bake for 25-30 minutes or until the chicken is cooked through and the cheese is bubbly.

Preparation Time: 15 minutes

Cooking Time: 25-30 minutes

Yield: 4 servings

Beer Cheese and Pretzel-Crusted Fish

Ingredients:
- 4 fish fillets (such as cod or haddock)
- 1 cup beer cheese sauce
- 2 cups crushed pretzels
- Cooking spray
- Lemon wedges, for serving

Instructions:
1. Preheat your oven to 400°F (200°C) and line a baking sheet with parchment paper.
2. Dip each fish fillet into the beer cheese sauce, allowing excess to drip off.
3. Coat the fish fillets with crushed pretzels and place them on the baking sheet.
4. Spray the tops of the fillets with cooking spray.
5. Bake for 15-20 minutes or until the fish is cooked and the pretzel crust is golden. Serve with lemon wedges.

Preparation Time: 15 minutes
Cooking Time: 15-20 minutes
Yield: 4 servings

Beer Cheese Mac 'n' Cheese

Ingredients:
- 12 oz elbow macaroni
- 2 cups beer cheese sauce
- 1/2 cup grated cheddar cheese
- 1/2 cup breadcrumbs
- Paprika and chopped fresh parsley, for garnish

Instructions:
1. Preheat your oven to 350°F (175°C).
2. Cook the macaroni according to the package instructions and drain.
3. In a large bowl, combine the cooked macaroni and beer cheese sauce.
4. Transfer the mixture to a baking dish, top with grated cheddar cheese, breadcrumbs, paprika, and parsley.
5. Bake for 20-25 minutes or until the top is golden and bubbly.

Preparation Time: 20 minutes
Cooking Time: 20-25 minutes
Yield: 6 servings

Beer Cheese Bratwurst Sandwiches

Ingredients:
- 4 bratwurst sausages
- 4 pretzel buns
- 1 cup beer cheese sauce
- 1 cup caramelized onions
- 1 cup sauerkraut
- Mustard, for serving

Instructions:
1. Grill the bratwurst sausages until cooked through.
2. Toast the pretzel buns on the grill.
3. Spread beer cheese sauce on the buns.
4. Place a grilled bratwurst on each bun and top with caramelized onions and sauerkraut.
5. Serve with mustard on the side.

Preparation Time: 15 minutes
Cooking Time: 15 minutes
Yield: 4 sandwiches

Beer Cheese and Broccoli-Stuffed Potatoes

Ingredients:
- 4 large russet potatoes
- 1 cup beer cheese sauce
- 2 cups steamed broccoli florets
- 1/2 cup cheddar cheese, grated
- Chopped chives, for garnish
- Sour cream, for serving (optional)

Instructions:
1. Preheat your oven to 375°F (190°C).
2. Bake the potatoes for 45-60 minutes or until tender.
3. Cut the tops off the potatoes and scoop out the flesh.
4. Mash the potato flesh with beer cheese sauce and steamed broccoli.
5. Refill the potato shells, sprinkle with cheddar cheese, and bake for another 10-15 minutes or until heated through and cheese is melted.
6. Garnish with chopped chives and serve with sour cream if desired.

Preparation Time: 15 minutes
Cooking Time: 75-80 minutes (including potato baking time)
Yield: 4 stuffed potatoes

Beer Cheese-Stuffed Burgers

Ingredients:
- 1.5 lbs ground beef
- 1 cup beer cheese sauce
- Salt and pepper, to taste
- Burger buns and your favorite toppings

Instructions:
1. Divide the ground beef into 8 equal portions.
2. Flatten each portion into a patty and spoon beer cheese sauce onto 4 of the patties.
3. Place the remaining 4 patties on top and seal the edges to encase the beer cheese.
4. Season the burgers with salt and pepper.
5. Grill the burgers over medium-high heat for 4-5 minutes per side or until they reach your desired level of doneness.
6. Serve on buns with your favorite toppings.

Preparation Time: 20 minutes
Cooking Time: 8-10 minutes
Yield: 4 stuffed burgers

Beer Cheese and Bacon-Wrapped Shrimp

Ingredients:
- 24 large shrimp, peeled and deveined
- 12 slices of bacon
- 1 cup beer cheese sauce
- Wooden skewers, soaked in water
- BBQ sauce, for basting

Instructions:
1. Preheat your grill to medium-high heat.
2. Wrap each shrimp with a slice of bacon and thread onto skewers.
3. Brush with BBQ sauce and grill for 2-3 minutes per side, or until the bacon is crispy and the shrimp are cooked.
4. Serve with a side of beer cheese sauce for dipping.

Preparation Time: 15 minutes
Cooking Time: 6-8 minutes
Yield: 4 servings

Beer Cheese and Bacon-Stuffed Mushrooms

Ingredients:
- 24 large mushroom caps
- 1 cup beer cheese sauce
- 12 slices of bacon
- Toothpicks

Instructions:
1. Preheat your oven to 375°F (190°C).
2. Wrap each mushroom cap with a slice of bacon and secure with a toothpick.
3. Place the mushrooms on a baking sheet and bake for 20-25 minutes until the bacon is crispy and the mushrooms are tender.
4. Serve with a side of beer cheese sauce for dipping.

Preparation Time: 15 minutes
Cooking Time: 20-25 minutes
Yield: 24 stuffed mushrooms

Beer Cheese Tacos

Ingredients:
- 1 lb boneless chicken breast or beef strips
- 1 cup beer cheese sauce
- 8 small flour tortillas
- Fresh salsa
- Sliced avocado
- Shredded lettuce

Instructions:
1. Cook the chicken or beef until done and season to taste.
2. Warm the tortillas.
3. Spread beer cheese sauce on each tortilla.
4. Add your choice of chicken or beef, and top with fresh salsa, sliced avocado, and shredded lettuce.
5. Roll up the tortillas and serve.

Preparation Time: 15 minutes
Cooking Time: Varies depending on meat choice
Yield: 4 servings

Beer Cheese-Stuffed Meatloaf

Ingredients:
- 2 lbs ground beef
- 1 cup beer cheese sauce
- 1 cup breadcrumbs
- 2 eggs
- 1/2 cup diced onions
- 1/2 cup diced bell peppers
- Salt and pepper, to taste
- Ketchup or barbecue sauce (for glaze)

Instructions:
1. Preheat your oven to 350°F (175°C).
2. In a large bowl, mix together the ground beef, beer cheese sauce, breadcrumbs, eggs, onions, bell peppers, salt, and pepper.
3. Shape the mixture into a loaf and place it in a baking dish.
4. Brush the top with ketchup or barbecue sauce.
5. Bake for 1 hour or until the meatloaf is cooked through.
6. Let it rest for a few minutes before slicing and serving.

Preparation Time: 20 minutes
Cooking Time: 1 hour
Yield: 6 servings

Side Dishes

1. **Beer Cheese Potato Wedges**: Crispy potato wedges coated with a savory beer cheese sauce, perfect for dipping.

2. **Beer Cheese Coleslaw**: A creamy and tangy coleslaw with a beer cheese twist, adding depth to the flavor.

3. **Beer Cheese Pretzel Bites**: Soft pretzel bites served with a warm beer cheese dip for a perfect pairing.

4. **Beer Cheese-Stuffed Mushrooms**: Mushroom caps filled with a delicious beer cheese stuffing, baked until tender.

5. **Beer Cheese Fries**: Classic French fries smothered in rich beer cheese sauce and garnished with scallions.

6. **Beer Cheese Bread**: A warm, pull-apart beer cheese bread that's great for sharing.

7. **Beer Cheese Rice**: Fluffy rice cooked in a beer cheese sauce, creating a comforting and creamy side dish.

8. **Roasted Brussels Sprouts with Beer Cheese Glaze**: Brussels sprouts roasted to perfection, then drizzled with a delectable beer cheese glaze.

9. **Beer Cheese Macaroni Salad**: A zesty macaroni salad with a creamy beer cheese dressing, ideal for barbecues and picnics.

10. **Beer Cheese Stuffed Peppers**: Bell peppers filled with a cheesy beer cheese mixture, baked until tender and bubbly.

These side dish recipes will add a delightful twist to your meals and complement your beer cheese-inspired dishes.

Beer Cheese Potato Wedges

Ingredients:
- 4 large russet potatoes, cut into wedges
- 1 cup beer cheese sauce
- Cooking oil
- Salt and pepper, to taste
- Fresh parsley, for garnish

Instructions:
1. Preheat your oven to 425°F (220°C).
2. Toss the potato wedges with cooking oil, salt, and pepper.
3. Arrange the wedges on a baking sheet and bake for 25-30 minutes, turning once, until they are golden and crispy.
4. Serve with a side of warm beer cheese sauce for dipping. Garnish with fresh parsley.

Preparation Time: 15 minutes
Cooking Time: 25-30 minutes
Yield: 4 servings

Beer Cheese Coleslaw

Ingredients:
- 4 cups shredded cabbage and carrots
- 1 cup beer cheese sauce
- 2 tablespoons mayonnaise
- 1 tablespoon apple cider vinegar
- 1 tablespoon honey
- Salt and pepper, to taste

Instructions:
1. In a large bowl, combine shredded cabbage and carrots.
2. In a separate bowl, whisk together beer cheese sauce, mayonnaise, apple cider vinegar, honey, salt, and pepper.
3. Pour the dressing over the coleslaw and toss to coat.
4. Chill in the refrigerator for at least 30 minutes before serving.

Preparation Time: 15 minutes
Chilling Time: 30 minutes
Yield: 4 servings

Beer Cheese Pretzel Bites

Ingredients:
- 1 batch of homemade or store-bought pretzel bites
- 1 cup beer cheese sauce
- Fresh chives, for garnish

Instructions:
1. Prepare the pretzel bites according to the recipe or package instructions.
2. Warm the beer cheese sauce.
3. Serve the pretzel bites with warm beer cheese sauce for dipping.
4. Garnish with fresh chives.

Preparation Time: Varies depending on pretzel bite preparation
Yield: Varies

Beer Cheese-Stuffed Mushrooms

Ingredients:
- 24 large mushroom caps
- 1 cup beer cheese sauce
- 2 tablespoons breadcrumbs
- 2 tablespoons fresh parsley, chopped

Instructions:
1. Preheat your oven to 375°F (190°C).
2. Fill each mushroom cap with beer cheese sauce.
3. In a small bowl, combine breadcrumbs and chopped parsley.
4. Sprinkle the breadcrumb mixture on top of the cheese-filled mushrooms.
5. Place the mushrooms on a baking sheet and bake for 15-20 minutes until the mushrooms are tender and the topping is golden.

Preparation Time: 15 minutes
Cooking Time: 15-20 minutes
Yield: 24 stuffed mushrooms

Beer Cheese Fries

Ingredients:
- 4 cups of French fries (homemade or frozen)
- 1 cup beer cheese sauce
- 2-3 scallions, chopped

Instructions:
1. Prepare the French fries according to the package or recipe instructions.
2. Warm the beer cheese sauce.
3. Drizzle the warm beer cheese sauce over the hot French fries.
4. Garnish with chopped scallions.

Preparation Time: Varies depending on French fry preparation
Yield: Varies

Beer Cheese Bread

Ingredients:
- 1 loaf of French bread or artisan bread
- 1 cup beer cheese sauce
- 2 tablespoons fresh parsley, chopped
- 2 tablespoons grated Parmesan cheese

Instructions:
1. Preheat your oven to 375°F (190°C).
2. Slice the bread lengthwise and spread beer cheese sauce evenly on the cut sides.
3. Reassemble the loaf and wrap it in aluminum foil.
4. Bake for 15-20 minutes or until the bread is hot and the cheese is bubbly.
5. Sprinkle with fresh parsley and grated Parmesan cheese before serving.

Preparation Time: 10 minutes
Cooking Time: 15-20 minutes
Yield: Varies

Beer Cheese Rice

Ingredients:
- 2 cups long-grain rice
- 4 cups chicken or vegetable broth
- 1 cup beer cheese sauce
- Fresh chives, for garnish

Instructions:
1. In a saucepan, bring the chicken or vegetable broth to a boil.
2. Stir in the rice, reduce the heat to low, cover, and simmer for 15-20 minutes or until the rice is tender.
3. Fluff the rice with a fork and stir in the beer cheese sauce.
4. Garnish with fresh chives before serving.

Preparation Time: 5 minutes
Cooking Time: 20-25 minutes (including rice preparation)
Yield: 4 servings

Roasted Brussels Sprouts with Beer Cheese Glaze

Ingredients:
- 1 lb Brussels sprouts, trimmed and halved
- 2 tablespoons olive oil
- Salt and pepper, to taste
- 1 cup beer cheese sauce
- Chopped bacon, for garnish (optional)

Instructions:
1. Preheat your oven to 400°F (200°C).
2. Toss the Brussels sprouts with olive oil, salt, and pepper.
3. Roast for 20-25 minutes until they are tender and crispy.
4. Warm the beer cheese sauce.
5. Drizzle the warm beer cheese sauce over the roasted Brussels sprouts.
6. Garnish with chopped bacon, if desired.

Preparation Time: 10 minutes
Cooking Time: 20-25 minutes
Yield: 4 servings

Beer Cheese Macaroni Salad

Ingredients:
- 8 oz elbow macaroni
- 1 cup beer cheese sauce
- 1/2 cup mayonnaise
- 1/4 cup diced red bell pepper
- 1/4 cup diced red onion
- 1/4 cup diced celery
- Salt and pepper, to taste

Instructions:
1. Cook the macaroni according to the package instructions and drain.
2. In a large bowl, combine the cooked macaroni, beer cheese sauce, mayonnaise, diced red bell pepper, red onion, celery, salt, and pepper.
3. Chill in the refrigerator for at least 30 minutes before serving.

Preparation Time: 15 minutes
Chilling Time: 30 minutes
Yield: 4 servings

Beer Cheese Stuffed Peppers

Ingredients:
- 4 large bell peppers (red, green, yellow, or orange)
- 1 cup beer cheese sauce
- Fresh parsley, for garnish

Instructions:
1. Preheat your oven to 375°F (190°C).
2. Cut the tops off the bell peppers and remove the seeds.
3. Fill each pepper with beer cheese sauce.
4. Place the peppers in a baking dish and bake for 30-35 minutes until the peppers are tender and the cheese is bubbly.
5. Garnish with fresh parsley before serving.

Preparation Time: 15 minutes
Cooking Time: 30-35 minutes
Yield: 4 stuffed peppers

Desserts

1. **Beer Cheese-Stuffed Pretzel Bites with Caramel Dip**: Soft pretzel bites filled with sweet beer cheese sauce and served with a luscious caramel dip.

2. **Beer Cheese Cheesecake**: A rich and creamy cheesecake with a beer cheese-infused filling and a graham cracker crust.

3. **Chocolate Beer Cheese Fondue**: A decadent chocolate fondue made with a blend of beer cheese, perfect for dipping fruits, marshmallows, and pretzels.

4. **Beer Cheese Apple Crisp**: Baked apple slices topped with a crumbly beer cheese and oat topping, served warm with a scoop of vanilla ice cream.

5. **Beer Cheese Chocolate Truffles**: Indulgent chocolate truffles filled with a beer cheese-infused ganache and coated with cocoa powder or crushed nuts.

6. **Beer Cheese Ice Cream**: Creamy beer cheese ice cream with a hint of sweetness, perfect for cooling down after a spicy meal.

7. **Beer Cheese Bread Pudding**: A delightful bread pudding made with chunks of beer cheese bread, drizzled with a warm beer cheese sauce.

8. **Beer Cheese Brownies**: Rich and fudgy brownies infused with beer cheese, offering a unique and delightful flavor.

9. **Beer Cheese Tiramisu**: A beer cheese twist on the classic Italian dessert, with layers of beer cheese-soaked ladyfingers and mascarpone cream.

10. **Beer Cheese Pie**: A sweet and savory pie with a beer cheese-infused filling, topped with whipped cream or a beer cheese drizzle.

These dessert recipes will add a unique and delightful ending to your beer cheese-inspired meals and gatherings.

Beer Cheese-Stuffed Pretzel Bites with Caramel Dip

Ingredients:
- 1 batch of homemade or store-bought pretzel bites
- 1 cup beer cheese sauce
- 1/2 cup caramel sauce

Instructions:
1. Prepare the pretzel bites according to the recipe or package instructions.
2. Warm the beer cheese sauce and caramel sauce.
3. Serve the pretzel bites with a side of warm beer cheese sauce and caramel sauce for dipping.

Preparation Time: Varies depending on pretzel bite preparation
Yield: Varies

Beer Cheese Cheesecake

Ingredients:
- 1 1/2 cups graham cracker crumbs
- 1/2 cup melted butter
- 2 cups cream cheese
- 1 cup beer cheese sauce
- 1 cup granulated sugar
- 1 tsp vanilla extract
- 4 large eggs
- Whipped cream and fresh berries for garnish (optional)

Instructions:

1. Preheat your oven to 325°F (160°C).

2. Combine graham cracker crumbs and melted butter, then press into the bottom of a 9-inch springform pan.

3. In a large bowl, beat cream cheese, beer cheese sauce, sugar, and vanilla until smooth.

4. Add eggs one at a time, beating well after each addition.

5. Pour the mixture over the crust.

6. Bake for 45-50 minutes or until the center is set.

7. Allow the cheesecake to cool, then refrigerate for at least 4 hours before serving.

8. Garnish with whipped cream and fresh berries if desired.

Preparation Time: 20 minutes

Cooking Time: 45-50 minutes

Chilling Time: 4 hours

Yield: 8 servings

Chocolate Beer Cheese Fondue

Ingredients:
- 8 oz dark chocolate, chopped
- 1 cup beer cheese sauce
- 1/4 cup heavy cream
- Assorted dippers (strawberries, marshmallows, pretzels, etc.)

Instructions:
1. In a saucepan, heat the beer cheese sauce and heavy cream until hot but not boiling.
2. Remove from heat and stir in the chopped dark chocolate until smooth.
3. Transfer the mixture to a fondue pot or a serving bowl.
4. Serve with assorted dippers for dipping.

Preparation Time: 10 minutes
Cooking Time: 5 minutes
Yield: 4 servings

Beer Cheese Apple Crisp

Ingredients:
- 4 cups sliced and peeled apples (such as Granny Smith)
- 1 cup beer cheese sauce
- 1 cup old-fashioned oats
- 1/2 cup all-purpose flour
- 1/2 cup brown sugar
- 1/2 cup unsalted butter, melted
- Vanilla ice cream for serving (optional)

Instructions:
1. Preheat your oven to 350°F (175°C).
2. In a large bowl, toss the sliced apples with beer cheese sauce and place in a baking dish.
3. In a separate bowl, combine oats, flour, brown sugar, and melted butter to create a crumbly topping.
4. Sprinkle the topping evenly over the apples.
5. Bake for 40-45 minutes or until the topping is golden and the apples are tender.
6. Serve warm, with a scoop of vanilla ice cream if desired.

Preparation Time: 15 minutes
Cooking Time: 40-45 minutes
Yield: 6 servings

Beer Cheese Chocolate Truffles

Ingredients:
- 8 oz dark chocolate, finely chopped
- 1/2 cup heavy cream
- 2 tablespoons beer cheese sauce
- Cocoa powder, crushed nuts, or sprinkles for coating

Instructions:
1. In a saucepan, heat the heavy cream and beer cheese sauce until it simmers.
2. Remove from heat and pour over the chopped dark chocolate.
3. Stir until the chocolate is completely melted and the mixture is smooth.
4. Chill the mixture in the refrigerator for at least 2 hours or until it's firm enough to handle.
5. Roll into small truffle-sized balls.
6. Roll each truffle in cocoa powder, crushed nuts, or sprinkles for coating.
7. Chill again before serving.
Preparation Time: 15 minutes
Chilling Time: 2 hours
Yield: Approximately 24 truffles

Beer Cheese Ice Cream

Ingredients:
- 2 cups heavy cream
- 1 cup whole milk
- 1 cup beer cheese sauce
- 1 cup granulated sugar
- 1 tsp vanilla extract

Instructions:

1. In a large mixing bowl, whisk together heavy cream, whole milk, beer cheese sauce, granulated sugar, and vanilla extract until well combined.

2. Pour the mixture into an ice cream maker and churn according to the manufacturer's instructions.

3. Transfer the ice cream to a lidded container and freeze for a few hours or until firm.

Preparation Time: 15 minutes

Churning and Freezing Time: Varies based on ice cream maker

Yield: 6 servings

Beer Cheese Bread Pudding

Ingredients:
- 6 cups cubed beer cheese bread
- 1 cup beer cheese sauce
- 2 cups milk
- 4 large eggs
- 1/2 cup granulated sugar
- 1 tsp vanilla extract
- Powdered sugar for dusting

Instructions:
1. Preheat your oven to 350°F (175°C).
2. Place the cubed beer cheese bread in a greased 9x13-inch baking dish.
3. In a bowl, whisk together beer cheese sauce, milk, eggs, granulated sugar, and vanilla extract.
4. Pour the mixture over the bread cubes, making sure all are evenly coated.
5. Let it sit for 15 minutes to allow the bread to absorb the liquid.
6. Bake for 45-50 minutes or until the pudding is set and the top is golden.
7. Dust with powdered sugar before serving.

Preparation Time: 15 minutes
Cooking Time: 45-50 minutes
Yield: 8 servings

Beer Cheese Brownies

Ingredients:
- 4 oz unsweetened chocolate, chopped
- 1/2 cup unsalted butter
- 1 cup granulated sugar
- 2 large eggs
- 1 tsp vanilla extract
- 1/4 cup beer cheese sauce
- 1/2 cup all-purpose flour
- 1/4 tsp salt

Instructions:
1. Preheat your oven to 350°F (175°C).
2. In a microwave-safe bowl, melt the unsweetened chocolate and butter in 30-second intervals, stirring until smooth.
3. In a separate bowl, whisk together sugar, eggs, and vanilla extract.
4. Stir in the melted chocolate mixture and beer cheese sauce.
5. Add the flour and salt, mixing until just combined.
6. Pour the batter into a greased 8x8-inch baking pan.
7. Bake for 25-30 minutes or until a toothpick comes out with a few moist crumbs.
8. Let the brownies cool before cutting into squares.

Preparation Time: 15 minutes
Cooking Time: 25-30 minutes
Yield: 16 brownies

Beer Cheese Tiramisu

Ingredients:
- 1 cup strong brewed coffee, cooled
- 1/4 cup coffee liqueur (optional)
- 1 cup beer cheese sauce
- 8 oz mascarpone cheese
- 1/2 cup powdered sugar
- 1 tsp vanilla extract
- 24 ladyfingers
- Cocoa powder for dusting

Instructions:
1. In a shallow dish, combine the brewed coffee and coffee liqueur.
2. In a separate bowl, whisk together beer cheese sauce, mascarpone cheese, powdered sugar, and vanilla extract until smooth.
3. Quickly dip each ladyfinger into the coffee mixture and arrange them in the bottom of a serving dish.
4. Spread half of the cheese mixture over the ladyfingers.
5. Repeat with another layer of dipped ladyfingers and the remaining cheese mixture.
6. Dust the top with cocoa powder.
7. Chill for at least 4 hours before serving.
Preparation Time: 20 minutes
Chilling Time: 4 hours
Yield: 8 servings

Beer Cheese Pie

Ingredients:
- 1 pie crust (homemade or store-bought)
- 1 cup beer cheese sauce
- 1 cup granulated sugar
- 2 large eggs
- 1 tsp vanilla extract
- Whipped cream for serving (optional)

Instructions:

1. Preheat your oven to 350°F (175°C).
2. Line a pie pan with the pie crust.
3. In a bowl, whisk together beer cheese sauce, granulated sugar, eggs, and vanilla extract.
4. Pour the mixture into the pie crust.
5. Bake for 30-35 minutes or until the filling is set and the crust is golden.
6. Allow the pie to cool before serving.
7. Top with whipped cream if desired.

Preparation Time: 10 minutes

Cooking Time: 30-35 minutes

Yield: 8 servings

Special Section

Appetizer Recipes:

Dietary Considerations:

- **Vegetarian Options**: Many of the appetizers are naturally vegetarian. Consider using vegetarian beer cheese for a fully vegetarian spread.

- **Gluten-Free Options**: Use gluten-free bread or crackers for dipping in beer cheese dips or spreads.

Meal Planning:

- **Variety is Key**: Choose a mix of hot and cold appetizers to cater to different tastes. Plan for 3-4 different appetizers for a well-rounded selection.

- **Preparation in Advance**: Many appetizers can be prepared partially in advance, making it easier to serve guests without being stuck in the kitchen.

Entertaining Tips:

- **Pairing with Beer**: Offer a selection of beer styles to pair with the appetizers, from light lagers to dark stouts.

- **Appetizer Platter**: Create a visually appealing platter with a variety of appetizers, garnished with fresh herbs or fruits.

Main Course Recipes:

Dietary Considerations:

- **Vegetarian Options**: Some main course recipes can be adapted with vegetarian proteins like tofu, tempeh, or meat substitutes.

- **Gluten-Free Options**: Serve main courses over gluten-free pasta, rice, or with gluten-free bread.

Meal Planning:

- **Balanced Courses**: Plan your main courses to include a balance of proteins, starches, and vegetables.

- **Scaling Up**: Adjust recipes to accommodate the number of guests and use a larger pan when preparing larger quantities.

Entertaining Tips:

- **Family-Style Dining**: Serve main courses family-style, allowing guests to pass dishes and engage in conversation.
- **Beer Pairing**: Offer a range of beer options that complement the flavors of the main dishes.

Side Dish Recipes:

Dietary Considerations:

- **Vegetarian Options**: Many side dishes are vegetarian, providing a variety of options for all guests.
- **Gluten-Free Options**: Substitute ingredients like gluten-free breadcrumbs or flour when necessary.

Meal Planning:

- **Complementary Sides**: Choose side dishes that complement the main course and add visual appeal to the table.
- **Balancing Flavors**: Incorporate side dishes with a mix of flavors and textures to create a well-rounded meal.

Entertaining Tips:

- **Timing**: Ensure side dishes are cooked and ready to serve along with the main course.
- **Garnish and Presentation**: Add fresh herbs, spices, or drizzles of beer cheese sauce for a finishing touch to your side dishes.

Dessert Recipes:

Dietary Considerations:

- **Vegetarian Options**: All dessert recipes are naturally vegetarian.
- **Gluten-Free Options**: Use gluten-free flour and ingredients to adapt dessert recipes.

Meal Planning:

- **Dessert Pairing**: Consider the sweetness of the dessert when selecting beer pairings. Opt for sweeter beers with dessert.

Entertaining Tips:

- **Dessert Buffet**: Create a dessert buffet with a variety of options, allowing guests to choose their favorites.
- **Coffee or Digestif**: Offer coffee or a digestif like liqueurs to accompany desserts for a perfect ending to the meal.

These special sections cater to dietary considerations, provide meal planning guidance, and offer entertaining tips to ensure your "Brews & Bites: A Beer Cheese Revolution" dining experience is a hit with all your guests, regardless of their preferences or dietary needs. Enjoy your culinary adventures!

Alphabetical Index:

A:

- **Apples**: Beer Cheese Apple Crisp (Dessert)

B:

- **Bread**: Beer Cheese Bread Pudding (Dessert)
- **Broth**: Beer Cheese Soup (Appetizer)
- **Brownies**: Beer Cheese Brownies (Dessert)

C:

- **Cheese**: Beer Cheese Sauce (Used in multiple recipes)
- **Chicken**: Beer Cheese Chicken Sliders (Main Course)

D:

- **Dips**: Beer Cheese Dips (Appetizer)
- **Desserts**: Various dessert recipes, including Beer Cheese Pie, Chocolate Beer Cheese Fondue, and more.
- **Dressings**: Beer Cheese Salad Dressing (Side)

F:

- **Fruit**: Used in various dessert recipes, such as Beer Cheese Apple Crisp.

G:

- **Garlic**: Used in various recipes, including beer cheese sauces and dips.
- **Grilled Meat**: Beer Cheese Grilled Chicken (Main Course)

I:

- **Ice Cream**: Beer Cheese Ice Cream (Dessert)

L:

- **Lager**: Beer Cheese Lager Soup (Appetizer)

M:

- **Meat**: Various meat options used in main course recipes, including chicken, beef, and more.

P:

- **Pasta**: Beer Cheese Pasta (Main Course)
- **Pretzel Bites**: Beer Cheese-Stuffed Pretzel Bites (Dessert)

S:
- **Salads**: Beer Cheese Salad (Side)
- **Sliders**: Beer Cheese Sliders (Main Course)
- **Soups**: Beer Cheese Soup (Appetizer)
- **Sweets**: Various dessert recipes
T:
- **Tiramisu**: Beer Cheese Tiramisu (Dessert)
- **Truffles**: Beer Cheese Chocolate Truffles (Dessert)
V:
- **Vegetables**: Used in various recipes, including soups, salads, and side dishes.
W:
- **Whipped Cream**: Used as a topping in some dessert recipes.

This alphabetical index will help you quickly locate key ingredients and their corresponding recipes in the "Brews & Bites: A Beer Cheese Revolution" cookbook, making it easier to plan and prepare your meals.

Conversion Charts

Measurement Conversions:

Volume:

- 1 teaspoon (tsp) = 5 milliliters (mL)
- 1 tablespoon (Tbsp) = 15 milliliters (mL)
- 1 fluid ounce (fl oz) = 30 milliliters (mL)
- 1 cup = 240 milliliters (mL)
- 1 pint = 480 milliliters (mL)
- 1 quart = 960 milliliters (mL)
- 1 gallon = 3,840 milliliters (mL)
- 1 liter (L) = 1,000 milliliters (mL)

Weight:

- 1 ounce (oz) = 28.35 grams (g)
- 1 pound (lb) = 453.59 grams (g)
- 1 gram (g) = 0.035 ounces (oz)
- 1 kilogram (kg) = 2.205 pounds (lb)

Temperature Conversions:

- Fahrenheit (°F) to Celsius (°C):
- (°F - 32) / 1.8 = °C
- Celsius (°C) to Fahrenheit (°F):
- (°C × 1.8) + 32 = °F

Ingredient Substitutions:

Common Ingredient Substitutions:

- **Buttermilk**: Mix 1 cup of milk with 1 tablespoon of lemon juice or vinegar as a buttermilk substitute.
- **Egg**: For baking, replace one egg with 1/4 cup of applesauce or 1/4 cup of yogurt. In savory dishes, use tofu or mashed bananas.
- **Heavy Cream**: Combine 3/4 cup of milk and 1/3 cup of butter to substitute for 1 cup of heavy cream.

- **All-Purpose Flour**: For gluten-free alternatives, try almond flour, coconut flour, or a gluten-free flour blend.
- **White Sugar**: Use honey, maple syrup, or agave nectar as a sweetener alternative.
- **Baking Powder**: Combine 1 part baking soda with 2 parts cream of tartar as a baking powder alternative.

Beer Cheese Ingredient Substitutions:

- **Beer Cheese Sauce**: If you prefer a non-alcoholic option, replace beer with chicken or vegetable broth in beer cheese recipes.

These measurement, temperature, and ingredient substitution tables are valuable references that will help you navigate the recipes in "Brews & Bites: A Beer Cheese Revolution" with ease and confidence in your kitchen.

Glossary

Culinary Terms:

1. **Mise en Place**: A French term that means "everything in its place." It refers to the practice of prepping and organizing all ingredients and tools before starting to cook, ensuring a smooth cooking process.

2. **Deglaze**: To add a liquid, such as wine or broth, to a hot pan with cooked bits of food (fond) to release their flavors and create a flavorful sauce.

3. **Sauté**: A cooking method where food is quickly cooked in a small amount of oil or butter over high heat. It's often used for vegetables or meats.

4. **Simmer**: To cook food gently in a liquid just below the boiling point, with small bubbles breaking the surface.

5. **Broil**: To cook by direct exposure to high, dry heat in an oven, typically from the top heating element. It's used to brown and crisp the top of dishes.

6. **Emulsify**: To combine two liquids, like oil and vinegar, that don't naturally mix by slowly adding one to the other while vigorously stirring.

Unfamiliar ingredients:

1. **Tempeh**: A plant-based protein made from fermented soybeans. It has a nutty flavor and firm texture, often used in vegetarian and vegan dishes.

2. **Mascarpone Cheese**: An Italian cream cheese with a rich, buttery flavor. It's a key ingredient in Tiramisu and some desserts.

3. **Cream of Tartar**: A white, powdery substance, a byproduct of winemaking, used as a stabilizing agent in baking, especially for whipped egg whites and meringues.

4. **Gouda**: A semi-hard cheese originating from the Netherlands, known for its creamy, mild, and slightly sweet flavor. It's used in various dishes.

5. **Tofu**: A soy-based protein made from coagulated soy milk. It has a neutral flavor and is often used in vegetarian and vegan cooking.

6. **Almond Flour**: Ground blanched almonds, used as a gluten-free alternative to wheat flour in baking and cooking.

7. **Coconut Flour**: A gluten-free flour made from dried and ground coconut meat, commonly used in gluten-free and paleo baking.

These definitions and explanations will help readers of "Brews & Bites: A Beer Cheese Revolution" understand and navigate the culinary terms and ingredients used in the cookbook, ensuring a successful and enjoyable cooking experience.

Don't miss out!

Visit the website below and you can sign up to receive emails whenever S.R. Moore publishes a new book. There's no charge and no obligation.

https://books2read.com/r/B-A-XIBBB-WTVPC

BOOKS 2 READ

Connecting independent readers to independent writers.

Did you love *Brews & Bites: A Beer Cheese Revolution*? Then you should read *Shamrock & Spoon: Modern Irish Cooking for Every Occasion*[1] by S.R. Moore!

[2]

"Shamrock & Spoon: Modern Irish Cooking for Every Occasion" invites you on a culinary journey through contemporary Irish cuisine. Elevate your St. Patrick's Day celebrations with innovative twists on classic dishes. From Guinness-infused stews to whiskey-glazed salmon, this cookbook offers gourmet recipes sure to impress. Discover the rich tapestry of Irish flavors and techniques, crafted for every occasion and palate. With detailed instructions and vibrant photography, embark on a gastronomic adventure that honors tradition while embracing creativity. Whether you're a seasoned chef or a home cook eager to explore new flavors, "Shamrock & Spoon" promises to inspire and delight with its sophisticated yet approachable approach to Irish cooking.

---

1. https://books2read.com/u/3k9X8N

2. https://books2read.com/u/3k9X8N

9 798215 890462